The Handbook for Leaders

"We strongly contend that most organizations are tapping only a fraction of the potential of their employees. We believe that people can rise to much higher levels of performance if the organization creates the proper climate."

"You will hear some people say that leadership development is something that organizations invest in for the long run, and that no one should expect an immediate payoff. We take exactly the opposite stance. You should be able to see results right away. If you do not see results relatively quickly, we doubt you ever will."

"Great leaders are defined by having a small number of strengths."

The Handbook
for Leaders

✓ 24 Lessons for
Extraordinary Leadership

JOHN H. ZENGER
JOSEPH FOLKMAN

MCGRAW-HILL
New York Chicago San Francisco Lisbon
London Madrid Mexico City Milan New Delhi
San Juan Seoul Singapore Sydney Toronto

The Handbook for Leaders: 24 lessons for extraordinary leadership

John H. Zenger, Joseph Folkman

ISBN 13: 978 007711624 8
ISBN 10: 0 07 711624 0

 **Professional**

Published by:
McGraw-Hill Publishing Company
Shoppenhangers Road,
Maidenhead,
Berkshire, England, SL6 2QL
Telephone: 44 (0) 1628 502500
Fax: 44 (0) 1628 770224
Website: www.mcgraw-hill.co.uk

British Library Cataloguing-in-Publication Data
A catalogue record of this book is available from the British Library.

McGraw-Hill books are available at special quantity discounts. Please contact the corporate sales executive.

Printed in Great Britain by Cromwell Press Ltd, Trowbridge, Wiltshire

The *McGraw·Hill* Companies

Contents

The Handbook for Leaders

☑ Extraordinary leadership

Should you care about developing your leadership skills? You should care. By developing your leadership skills, you are assured a more rewarding and successful career. You will make a greater difference in every organization in which you work. You will lift the performance of everyone who works with you. If you aspire to greater responsibility and the rewards that follow, then learning how to be a better leader is a necessary step to getting there. Opportunities and rewards in your organization will surely increase if you are an effective leader.

Your organization (whether a hospital, a government agency, a business, or a school) needs you to be a strong and effective leader. Research presented in this book proves there is a high correlation between leadership effectiveness and the results that leaders produce. Developing an adequate cadre of leaders to perpetuate their organization is the number one preoccupation of CEOs in today's large corporations.

What's more, your organization needs you to be more than "adequate" in your leadership. While those who learn to lead get better results than those who don't, one startling conclusion presented in this book is the huge difference between the merely good and the extraordinary leader.

Unfortunately, the concept of leadership continues to be shrouded in misunderstanding. Ask 100 people to define leadership, and you are sure to get 100 different responses. So one objective of this book is to provide a simple and practical definition of leadership. It is not based on the subjective impressions of the authors but comes from solid empirical research.

Based on analysis of over 20,000 leaders, this book describes the 16 behaviors that differentiate the best leaders from the least effective. These are the behaviors that subordinates, peers, and bosses notice. These are the behaviors that you should work on developing.

Many leaders mistakenly believe that the path to greatness lies in finding their least effective traits or skills and then bringing those so-called "weaknesses" up into an acceptable range. These leaders believe that by removing these lower scores, they will be perceived as much more effective leaders. This book argues that this is a grave misconception.

Great leaders are defined by their having a small number of real strengths. Exceptional leaders don't become successful because they are flawless. And, conversely, they are not exceptional leaders because they do 180 things remarkably well. This book describes how the acquisition of certain strengths helps make you an extraordinary leader. These strengths can catapult leaders into the 90th percentile. Those people then make enormous contributions to the success of their organizations and their employees. The following lessons are stepping stones you can follow to become an extraordinary leader.

"Great leaders are not defined by the absence of weakness, but rather by the presence of clear strengths. The key to developing great leadership is to build strengths."

☐ ~~Leaders are born~~

☑ **Leaders can be made**

When the subject turns to leadership, someone inevitably asks, "Isn't leadership something you either have or you don't? Aren't leaders born that way? Can people really become leaders?" These questions are as hardy as cockroaches—they just won't die.

In fact, leadership characteristics can be developed. You can be a better leader. It is true that some leadership characteristics show up very early in life, but it is also true that people often can't predict who will become the superstar leaders. Some people come into the world endowed with self-confidence and a keen intellect. That is clearly an advantage. But nearly all people are made better leaders from specific developmental activities. Leaders are a lot more "made" than they are "born."

One of the best evidence that leaders can be created starting with "regular" people is the remarkable track record of the U.S. Marines. Marine recruits often come from troubled or abusive homes. They are frequently casual users of drugs or alcohol or have minor convictions. They often have not attended college. All the usual predictors of success are generally absent in this group of individuals. Yet many marine recruits are transformed into effective leaders after a two- to three-year period and go on to display remarkable leadership skills as their careers continue.

Leadership experts James Kouzes and Barry Posner wrote, "We would be intellectually dishonest if we did not say that some individuals clearly have a higher probability of succeeding at leadership than others. But this does not mean that ordinary managers cannot become extraordinary leaders." Leadership potential can be developed. With effort and practice, you can move beyond the skills you're born with to be an excellent leader.

Our goal in writing *The Handbook for Leaders* was to demystify the concept of leadership—to clarify what it takes to be an extraordinary leader. To do this, we examined what real people say about real leaders. We looked at evaluations of 20,000 leaders who had been assessed by 200,000 bosses, colleagues, and employees. We compared the top 10 percent of these leaders with the bottom 10 percent to see what leadership characteristics made the difference. This book shares some of our insights from our more detailed book, *The Extraordinary Leader*.

To build your leadership skills:

Believe that ordinary managers can become extraordinary: Your mindset can make the difference.

Commit to learning the concepts in this book: The more you know about what makes a leader extraordinary, the better your chances are of being phenomenal.

Try out the skills: Incorporate these ideas into action. Make yourself a better leader.

"The most dangerous leadership myth is that leaders are born—that there is a genetic factor to leadership. Myth asserts that people simply either have certain charismatic qualities or not. That's nonsense; in fact, the opposite is true. Leaders are made rather than born."

—Warren G. Bennis

☐ ~~Leaders don't matter~~

☑ Great leaders make a great difference

In our research we found conclusive evidence that leaders with poor leadership skills generate poor results. That finding will not come as a shock. It is quite intuitive to anyone who has worked in an organization for more than a few weeks. And our research is equally clear about the fact that good leaders tend to produce good results for their organizations.

What's more, most individuals do not need sophisticated measurement tools to tell the difference between good leaders and bad leaders. They feel the difference. They have experienced the effects at a very personal level. In general, good leaders are more effective than bad leaders in almost every dimension. Great leaders improve productivity, reduce turnover, enhance customer service, and create high levels of employee commitment.

Our research shows that there is another, even more dramatic, level of difference between *good* and *extraordinary* leaders. This was a major surprise finding of our research. Extraordinary leaders make a major difference, when compared with merely good leaders. They create even less turnover, motivate employees to perform at a much higher level, and greatly enhance customer satisfaction.

One analysis, combining results from dozens of studies, showed that for high-level jobs, the productivity difference between the top performers and the great majority is huge. Results showed that the top person is *127 percent more productive* than the average person and *infinitely more productive* than the 100th person in that curve.

Our goal was to examine just how powerful an extraordinary leader's effect could be, particularly on the bottom line. In one mortgage bank, we found that "extraordinary" leaders created profits that were nearly double those of the merely "good" leaders. In another study, organizations with excellent leaders had average stock returns nearly seven times higher than the general market.

To increase a leader's positive impact:

Focus on moving leaders from "bad" to "good": Poor leaders drive customers and employees away. They lose money for their businesses. *On every measurable dimension of organizational performance, good leaders outperform bad.*

Don't focus on moving leaders from "good" to "slightly better": There is not much difference in outcomes between leaders ranked in the middle categories—from the 30th to the 70th percentile. Making small, incremental improvements in leadership effectiveness in this range does not seem to substantially affect organizational outcomes.

Set the goal of moving leaders from "good" to "great": Huge differences exist between top performers and average performers for all types of jobs in every outcome category. If leaders can move from the "good" level to the "extraordinary" level at a reasonable cost to the organization, the return on that investment will be substantial.

"Extraordinary leaders . . . consistently achieve results that far exceed those of the good leaders."
—John H. Zenger and Joseph Folkman

☐ Go for good leaders

☑ Make good leaders great

One of the major failings of many leadership development programs is that they don't expect enough. Michelangelo stated, "The greatest danger for most of us is *not that our aim is too high and we miss it*, but that it is *too low and we reach it*."

Too many good leaders feel that being good is "good enough." They don't believe that they are personally capable of achieving superstar levels of performance. They believe that extraordinary leaders are prodigies, having been endowed with some unusual gifts from birth. They watch amazing leaders the way many people watch concert pianists and think, "It would be fun to be that good, but I could never do it. I just don't have that much talent."

However, innate natural talent is *not* the best predictor of who will become the excellent concert artists—or the extraordinary leaders. What makes the difference is *discipline*.

As one professor explained, "Discipline is always more important than some natural ability. With some dedicated practice, those with discipline will surpass those with natural ability in a few semesters. Without discipline and the ability to learn, those with natural ability will never progress above their current ability." In fact, there is quite a bit of evidence that shows that concert musicians are as good as they are simply because they have practiced two to four hours a day for over 10 years. They just had the interest and discipline to do it!

Most individuals, as they become managers for the first time, go through an intense learning period. They receive a great deal of training and personal coaching and are open to ideas and suggestions from experienced managers. They take time to plan meetings and performance reviews and how they will give feedback to direct reports. They also pay close attention to others, watching to understand techniques and skills. They are practicing leadership with the intent to get better. Their learning curve is steep.

Once they get reasonably competent at being managers, they switch from practicing to playing. Playing at leadership is inherently more fun, but skill development is very slow and sometimes stops altogether.

To improve everyone's leadership ability:

Push for improvement from everyone: Blaming bad leaders for the company's woes is too simple. Accept the need for *everyone* to undertake some level of improvement.

Take an interest: Why are some students willing to practice longer and harder? The key difference does not seem to be ability, but interest. Become an astute observer of leadership and implement what you see modeled.

Practice—don't play—at leadership: Bad leaders assume that deliberate practice makes no difference, so they continue to perform, but they never improve. Good leaders keep their focus and continue to build skills long after they achieve an adequate level of performance.

"If better is possible, good is not enough."
—Unknown

☐ Focus on leadership traits

☑ Raise the leadership "tent"

For decades, leadership experts have tried to find the list of distinctive traits that define great leaders. They assumed that each trait *stands alone*, much like the individually encased coil springs in an expensive mattress. As the advertisements demonstrate, if a bowling ball is dropped on one coil over here, the cup of water on the coil over there will not spill a drop. This metaphor suggests that leadership skills are solitary and independent, not intertwined, as we believe they are.

A more accurate metaphor for understanding leadership is a large tent, with the three-dimensional space under the canvas representing leadership effectiveness. *The poles in our metaphor represent key "strengths" of the individual leader*, especially those five that have been shown to make a difference in separating the great from the good: 1. *char-*

acter, 2. *personal capability*, 3. *focus on results*, 4. *interpersonal skills*, and 5. *leading organizational change*. The tent canvas represents all the possible competencies a leader might display.

The key to becoming a more effective leader is to lift more of the tent by hoisting multiple poles in the air. Lifting one tent pole pulls the entire tent up around that pole and raises a broad expanse of canvas. As a second competency pole is lifted, a new section of the tent is elevated, which not only raises the canvas above it, but also raises the canvas between the two leadership poles. With each succeeding competency tent pole, large expanses of canvas are lifted, until ultimately there is a huge volume of space under the tent.

Some strategies for raising the leadership tent:

Develop critical competencies: Seek to be competent in each of the five leadership areas.

Develop a combination of competencies: The canvas will not be raised with just one or two competency poles in the air. Great leaders need a balance of complementary skills.

More is better: Leaders with strengths in each of the five areas will hoist the most impressive tents.

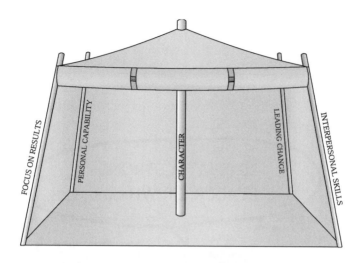

"Leadership behaviors are all knit together, much like the complex network of the human brain. There is an unbelievable interdependence between them."

—John H. Zenger and Joseph Folkman

☐ ~~Character doesn't matter~~

☑ Character is the essence of leadership

The central tent pole in our leadership metaphor is *character*. Our research shows that a person who receives low marks on character has *absolutely no chance* of being perceived as a great leader, especially in the long run. Leaders who lack character must constantly be on guard that people will discover the truth about them. Like the Hollywood set that looks real from one side, they live in constant danger of having the illusion of their character dispelled if others see behind the façade.

What are the key elements of strong personal character? Leaders with character follow through on commitments. They keep their word. They make decisions with the good of the organization in mind, rather than a personal agenda. These leaders gain respect by being open and transparent. In fact, the more people can see inside, the more highly regarded the leader will be.

Leaders with character treat others with respect. They don't "smile up and kick down." The bellhop and the waitress get the same consideration as the CEO. Leaders with integrity look at others through a positive lens. They assume others have good intentions rather than bad. They look to collaborate rather than compete.

High-character leaders keep learning. They try new things and adjust rapidly to changing environments. They attempt to improve themselves constantly. They look for feedback and act on it.

Surely some must be wondering, "But can I *improve* my character? If so, how?" The answer might be surprising. Some believe the following chain of events is typical:

Character ⇨ Attitudes ⇨ Behavior

This sequence assumes you must first will your character into a new state; then your attitudes and behavior will follow. *But the fact is that people work very hard to make their attitudes, and ultimately their character, conform to their behavior.* If you successfully alter your behavior, there will be a remarkable transformation in attitudes and, eventually, character. In essence, we believe the following chain better maps reality:

Behavior ⇨ Attitudes ⇨ Character

We suggest the following steps to alter behaviors and ultimately character:

Always deliver: Be cautious in the commitments you make. Be careful not to overstate or over-promise what you can accomplish. Follow through. If you know you won't be able to keep a commitment, don't brush it under the rug. Admit it and reclarify your intentions.

Be humble: Be willing to laugh at yourself. Don't flaunt your authority. Humility will make you approachable. It opens the door to building relationships.

Find a mirror: You need to find out how others perceive your character. This mirror may be a good internal mentor, a trusted colleague or friend, or an effective 360-degree feedback process. Without this self-critical perspective, it is impossible to exert strong influence on a work group.

"Everything about great leadership radiates from character."

—Dave Ulrich

☐ Leaders just need to lead

☑ Leaders need personal capability

The second critical tent pole of leadership is the *personal capabilities* the leader possesses. *These personal capabilities are not skills that would typically be described as leadership skills*, yet our research proves they must be in place for any individual to be perceived as a strong leader. Here are some of these individual capabilities:

- *Technical knowledge.* The best leaders have at least a working knowledge of the technological side of the business.
- *Product knowledge.* Great leaders need a thorough understanding of what the organization produces and why it is superior to competitive products.
- *Problem analysis and problem-solving skills.* These skills include the ability to define prob-

lems, analyze them, and come up with solid recommendations for resolving complex issues.

- *Professional skills.* Excellent leaders must be able to write intelligently and concisely, make compelling presentations, organize their work efficiently, monitor progress, and work without close supervision.

- *Innovation.* This refers to a leader's ability to have a fresh outlook in approaching a problem, to shake loose from old methods, and see new possibilities.

- *Initiative.* The best leaders see when something is falling through the cracks and immediately step in to make certain it is handled.

- *Effective use of information technology.* Great leaders set an example in the consistent use of e-mail, powerful software applications, and any technology that escalates performance.

Career experts Gene Dalton and Paul Thompson explain that the most successful leaders progress through a series of *four career stages that cannot be skipped.* Stage one is the time when individuals must prove they can learn the business and develop a solid foundation of technical expertise. In stage two, individuals continue to build technical skills and become *independent contributors.* By stage three, they become *mentors*—developing the careers and expertise of others. In stage four, they become *orga-*

nizational visionaries—leading the organization in new directions.

Too often, leaders reach a position they've been seeking and start to coast—believing that the learning phase of their career is over. They assume that there is a time for learning and a time for execution, and they are done learning. The best leaders *never* quit learning.

Here are some techniques to maximize your personal capability:

Understand the technology: Employees can see through attempts to cover up your lack of knowledge. Get up to speed by asking questions. Be willing to admit what you don't know.

Perfect professional skills: Managers can't manage unless they can communicate.

Try new things: Great managers innovate and take initiative. They think outside the box and don't hesitate to experiment.

"Leadership cannot be delegated to others."
—John H. Zenger and Joseph Folkman

☐ ~~Ignore the bottom line~~

☑ Focus on results

Leadership is ultimately about *producing results*. This is the third leadership tent pole. Leaders can have talent and character, but unless they produce sustained, impressive results for their organization, they simply are not good leaders.

One study of 1,000 managers showed that the best managers translate ideas into action. They push to take the next step forward by bringing energy, enthusiasm, and urgency to their role. They continually look for ways to improve. These leaders are in the driver's seat, with a foot on the accelerator—pressed to the floorboard most of the time.

How do leaders focus on results? Extraordinary leaders do the following:

- Establish stretch goals for their people.
- Take personal responsibility for the outcomes of the group.

- Provide ongoing feedback and coaching to their people.
- Set lofty targets for the group to achieve.
- Personally sponsor an initiative or action.
- Initiate new programs, projects, processes, client relationships, or technology.
- Focus on organization goals and ensure that they are translated into actions by their department.
- Operate with speed and intensity; accelerate the pace of the group.
- Champion the cause of the customer.
- Balance long-term and short-term objectives.

The best leaders get things accomplished, even under duress. They choose the right goals and follow through.

These are some ways to bring about results:

Know what the organization expects: Ask, "What does the organization expect from my department?" "From me personally?" The answers can be quite eye-opening.

Stay focused on long-term results: We've all seen executives who can make earnings soar—temporarily. Extraordinary leaders resist the urge to sacrifice long-term for short-term results. They keep the welfare of the organization ahead of their own personal agendas.

Take action: Extraordinary leaders wake up in the morning with a plan and put it into effect. They don't always wait for permission before moving ahead. Instead, they simply try new things.

"Leaders who aren't getting results aren't truly leading."
—David Ulrich, Jack Zenger, and Norm Smallwood

☐ ~~Nice guys finish last~~

☑ Cultivate interpersonal skills

The fourth essential tent pole of leadership is *interpersonal skills*. Along with the central tent pole representing character, it probably holds the most canvas. This leadership skill has become more important over time, especially since the demise of the "command and control" styles of leadership. Of all the competencies, interpersonal skills seem to make the most difference in whether leaders are considered extraordinary.

To develop strong interpersonal skills, leaders must do the following:

Communicate powerfully and prolifically. Extraordinary leaders don't hoard new insights. They tell people! These leaders give their work group a sense of direction and purpose. They help people understand how their work contributes to the goals of the organization. They err on the side of telling people too much.

Inspire others to high performance. Great leaders energize people to go the extra mile. They set stretch goals that motivate people to accomplish more than they think is possible.

Build trust. Superstar leaders act so that others trust them. They balance their concern for productivity and results with sensitivity to employees' needs and problems. When conflicts arise, they deal with employees' feelings as well as the technical aspects of the issue. They stay approachable.

Develop others. The most remarkable leaders support others' growth by giving honest and constructive feedback, balancing corrective with positive evaluations. They stay tuned to what is happening in employees' careers. They let others grow, even if it means letting them leave the department.

Collaborate and develop strong teams. Excellent leaders know not to insulate themselves from other team members and departments. They keep in touch, so that cooperative urges beat out competitive urges. They cultivate their team members' ability to work with diverse people.

Some key points for mastering people skills include:

Involve others in communication: One of the best ways to communicate is to get others to communicate! Interestingly, the worst communicators focus solely on getting their message across. The best communicators check people's reactions and get their ideas.

Train everyone to be a leader: These days, leadership often gets passed around in a group. The person with the loftiest title and supposed power is no longer the one with all the answers. Believe that others are capable of great accomplishments and then watch them follow through.

To develop others, develop yourself: The best leaders create space for their employees to move up from below by raising their own performance. Their efforts not only set the example, but also blaze a clear path for others to follow.

"If we treat people as they are, we make them worse, but if we treat them as they ought to be, we help them become what they are capable of becoming."

—Johann Wolfgang von Goethe

☑ Lead organizational change

The *ability to lead organizational change* is the fifth tent pole of extraordinary leadership. The best leaders inspire people to rally around a change, while poor leaders have to push, cajole, or even threaten employees to accept change. A turbulent business environment puts leaders to the test: Excellent leaders can turn a significant change into a pleasant journey, while poorly led change might be better described as a "trip through hell." With most organizations today in a constant state of change—from dramatic growth to downsizing and restructuring—leaders must be able to skillfully shepherd organizations in new strategic directions.

We're not talking about slight tactical shifts in current management processes or procedures. Caretaker managers can keep things going on a steady path. But if the organization is to rise to a significantly higher level of performance, extraordinary leaders must be able to sense the direction of the market and alter the fundamental business model. They must be able to envision and create a new organization culture.

How do extraordinary leaders approach this task? The challenge in accomplishing change is not only to provide strong direction, but also to get people involved in making the change work. The most effective leaders are able to strike a balance between directing change and involving others.

Leaders with strong directing tendencies are often prepared with well-organized plans that they communicate clearly. They maintain control, but they sometimes end up with employees feeling that changes are being done *to* them and not *with* them. The end result is that employees resist change and start to distrust management.

On the other hand, leaders who favor involving others in change sometimes fail to provide *enough* direction, leaving employees confused about their roles and what they need to do to keep the change moving forward. Sometimes leaders who tend toward involving others are simply unwilling to take risks or make tough decisions.

Our research shows clearly that both sets of behaviors are necessary for a leader to manage change effectively. Leaders need to help their people understand the specific details of the change and also help them feel involved so they will feel committed to the change.

Leading organizational change requires that you:

Create the overarching vision: Using your knowledge of the external environment, determine which trends to pursue and which to ignore. Stay involved in critical decisions. Use your influence to shape their outcome.

Translate the vision into specific objectives: In order to make the strategic vision happen, break it down to the level of specific tasks and expectations for individual workers. It is up to you to determine how resources will be allocated. You must establish the norms that will shape the culture.

Balance the need for direction with the need to involve others: Build support for your vision by getting people onboard.

"Some people grin and bear it. Others smile and change it."

—Unknown

☐ ~~Follow the leadership formula~~

☑ Find your leadership "sweet spot"

A psychologist once observed that the secret to life is discovering what "instrument" you are and then learning to play it. Woodwinds are no better than brass, nor are cellos superior to kettledrums. Each does something extremely well, and the musical score requires each unique contribution.

As individuals, we all have competencies and abilities that come to us more easily than others. We are drawn to some tasks and resist others. It is not difficult to see that, in any group of leaders, there are marked individual differences. One key to extraordinary leadership is finding the intersection of what you do well, what you love doing, and what the organization values.

One of our colleagues, Kurt Sandholtz, wanted to learn what causes people to have a "career best" experience—a time when they felt they were making a significant contribution and were very successful. After asking thousands of people, "What is the best job you've ever had?" he found that "career bests" have three common characteristics:

1. "Career bests" tap into a person's talents or competencies. When people are performing their best, they are almost always using skills, knowledge, or expertise that sets them apart from others.

2. A "career best" experience builds on what people are passionate about. Passions are things we love to do, regardless of how well we do them. For example, some love to sing in the shower, despite knowing they do not do it well.

3. "Career bests" inevitably add value to the organization. When people describe their ultimate career experiences, they don't say, "I was very competent and loved doing this job, but no one in the organization noticed."

When you find the area of intersection of your competencies, your passion, and organizational needs, you will find that you feel more engaged and motivated and that work is just more fun. In addition, you will be adding more value than your colleagues— and your performance ratings will reflect that.

To find your personal leadership "sweet spot":

Determine your strengths and passions: Ask yourself these questions. What do I do extremely well? When people talk about my abilities, what do they mention first? What activities energize me and bring me a great deal of personal satisfaction?

Determine what your organization values: Just as personalities are unique, so too are organizations. Look for what your organization needs. If it doesn't fit with what you enjoy and do well, look for an organization that *does* need what you have to offer.

Find the area of intersection: Extraordinary leaders find the spot where their competencies and passion overlap with an organizational need. This creates an opportunity for them to be and do their best.

"We are not in a position in which we have nothing to work with. We already have capacities, talents, direction, missions, callings."

—Abraham Maslow

☐ ~~Eliminate the rough edges first~~

☑ **Focus on building strengths**

Let's imagine that you have a renewed determination to improve your leadership effectiveness. To start the process, you participate in a 360-degree assessment of your competencies. In our experience, when people get feedback on their behavior, they always seem compelled to focus their attention on the items with the lowest scores. Something in our culture drives us to completely ignore our higher scores and shine a spotlight on the lowest ones.

Most people believe that fixing weaknesses will have a more powerful impact on leadership effectiveness ratings than building strengths. Where does this belief come from? Perhaps we learned it in school. After all, our teachers spent a lot more time correcting mistakes than focusing on what we did well. Or perhaps we feel compelled to be "renaissance people," with remarkable talent in every area. Perhaps our performance appraisal process of focusing primarily on deficiencies rather than strengths is to blame.

Ultimately, however, this strategy is not the most helpful for getting leaders from good to great. *What is much more effective in the long run is to focus on building strengths.* Peter Drucker once wrote: "Most problems cannot be solved. Most problems can only be survived. And one survives problems by making them irrelevant because of success.... One focuses on success, especially on unexpected success, and runs with it."

Here are some strategies for staying focused on strengths rather than weaknesses:

Understand that weaknesses sometimes deserve to be ignored: We can't all be Mary Poppins, famous for being "practically perfect in every way." If you've never been good at math, it's unlikely you'll be an engineer any time soon.

Improve at what you do well: You will get more mileage out of focusing on your areas of expertise and skill. Make them even better!

Look for the strengths in others: If you want to get your employees from good to great, try encouraging them in their areas of talent.

"Do not think of your faults: look for what is good and strong and try to imitate it. Your faults will drop off like dead leaves, when the time comes."

—John Ruskin

☐ ~~Seek perfection~~

☑ Concentrate on developing three to five strengths

Imagine receiving the results of a 360-degree assessment that shows your ratings as slightly above average on all competencies. You may feel relatively pleased. But you might not be so pleased if your child came home from school with all C+'s on his or her report card. Our research shows that just a few strengths can have a dramatic positive effect on the perception of a leader's effectiveness—but only when a competency stands out.

We wanted to understand how strengths affect overall leadership effectiveness, so we asked people, "What would you guess the overall effectiveness percentile would be for people with no strengths?" Most people indicated they thought a leader with no noteworthy strengths would be rated on average at the 50th percentile. However, our study of 8,000 leaders shows these leaders actually received ratings at the 34th percentile. *In other words, possessing no strengths plunges you to the bottom third in terms of perceived overall leadership effectiveness.*

Why are leaders with no area of strength perceived to be in the bottom third? It's because they lack a redeeming quality, skill, or ability. They may not be *ineffective* at anything, but they also are not terribly *effective* at anything. Leaders with just one strength move from the 34th percentile to the 64th percentile, on average. *Imagine, a 30 percent increase just for possessing one strength!* This shows the powerful influence of being good at any one competency.

Our research shows that leaders with three strengths are rated at the 81st percentile, while leaders with five strengths rank in the top 10 percent—at the 91st percentile. When we have challenged leaders to move from the 50th percentile to the 90th percentile, their response was most often that it seemed impossible. Their perception was that they would need to be perfect in almost every competency to achieve such a high rating. That clearly is not so. We found that *to be at the 90th percentile simply requires a leader to be highly skilled at five competencies!* This seems achievable to most aspiring leaders.

To improve in a manageable number of areas:

Push yourself to improve: Possessing even one strength causes performance ratings to improve drastically.

Don't overextend: There are limits to what you can accomplish. Don't try to change everything at once. We suggest you focus on improving in no more than three areas at a time.

Focus on getting to great: Becoming an extraordinary leader is not impossible. The first step is knowing where to concentrate your energies.

"People can only be successful at change if they focus their effort in a few areas. We recommend a maximum of three areas of improvement at any one time."

—John H. Zenger and Joseph Folkman

☑ Let the halo effect work for you

One of our most interesting findings was that *some leaders seemed to be able to do no wrong*. These remarkable leaders tended to be rated at the 90th percentile on almost all competencies. Simultaneously, *some leaders could do no right*. Their ratings fell in the lowest percentile on almost all competencies. We believe that both sets of ratings are a distortion.

When leaders perform extraordinarily well on a few behaviors, people's impressions of them on other competencies tend to be distorted positively. The opposite effect seems to occur for those with a few profound weaknesses. The halo effect can be a useful tool for those seeking to improve their leadership skills.

We have all seen the halo effect in action. How many times have we been disappointed to hear a speech by a famous actor or athlete? Why did we believe that he or she would have something insightful or even interesting to say? Just because a person can act or play sports does not mean he or she will have wisdom to share on other topics. We see the effect on the negative side when we demonize people who have made serious mistakes.

One explanation for the halo effect comes from fascinating research by Leon Festinger. Festinger describes how people experience tension when they believe two contradictory ideas, such as "My manager is a terrible leader" and "My manager is very good at solving complex and difficult problems." Hundreds of experiments have shown that people will do whatever is necessary to reduce the dissonance between conflicting ideas. When leaders improve their abilities in a few competencies, this creates a potentially useful dissonance in the minds of others. People ask themselves, "How can this leader be so effective on some things but less effective on others?" People then close the gap on the dissonance by shifting their beliefs. They assume leaders are more competent than they truly are, creating a positive effect for leaders who develop extraordinary strengths.

To take advantage of this halo effect:

Build up a few profound strengths: Not only will your strengths help produce positive results, they will also create a powerful impression of competence.

Be great at what your organization cares about: You will get the most mileage from your strengths if they're in areas that are highly valued. If your organization cares most about excellent communication skills, make sure you communicate clearly!

Let people know your talents: While you don't want to alienate people by showing off, you do want to let people know your capabilities. The more they know your strengths, the more pressure they will feel to assume you have strengths in other areas too.

"If people have the general impression that a person is an extraordinary leader, they will over-estimate this person's skills and abilities. The key is to get the attribution process to work for you rather than against you."
—John H. Zenger and Joseph Folkman

☐ Build one skill at a time

☑ Look for powerful combinations of competencies

Brett Savage, a long-time colleague, told the secret of his success playing high school football. Brett had two attributes on his side. One was his height of 6 feet 4 inches, more the physique of a basketball player than a football player. The second was his ability to catch anything thrown anywhere close to him. Every time Brett went out for a pass, all the quarterback had to do was throw the ball just a little over Brett's head and the defensive backs were helpless to prevent him from catching it. As Brett explained, "The combination of height and good hands was powerful."

We were interested to see the impact of combinations of competencies on leadership ratings. To research this, we examined leaders who had been rated in the top 25 percent for interpersonal skills but were rated below the top quartile for focus on results. When we examined this group, we found that only 9 percent of these people were also rated as excellent leaders. Clearly, interpersonal skills alone do not guarantee a high ranking on leadership.

When we examined those leaders who were ranked high in *both* interpersonal skills and focus on results, this group was *much more likely to be ranked as excellent leaders*. With both areas of expertise, these individuals now had a 66 percent chance of being ranked as excellent leaders! Both skills are valuable and lead to success, but the *combination* of being excellent at both skills together substantially increased the probability of overall effectiveness.

The secret to building success as a leader is to be excellent at powerful combinations of skills. We have found that there are many such powerful combinations. Some of the most useful combinations include personal skills in getting the work done coupled with the ability to encourage others to perform their work. The effect of powerful combinations is to erect and lengthen the tent poles that lift the overall leadership tent to new heights.

Here are some examples of these combinations:

- Technical knowledge and the ability to inspire or motivate others.

- Connecting with the outside world and the ability to inspire and motivate others.
- Focus on results and the ability to communicate powerfully and prolifically.
- Teamwork/collaboration and establishing stretch goals.
- Strategic perspective and problem-solving/analytical skills.

Some helpful methods for building combinations of competencies include:

Build complementary skills: Look for ways to improve on skills that work together to produce a whole greater than the sum of the parts.

Do some research: You can contact the authors at www.expgi.com to learn how to find out more about these powerful combinations. Determine which areas of improvement will best serve you.

Cross train: Sometimes the best way to strengthen one competency is to focus on another. You may want to first tackle skills that you are more likely to improve easily.

"Powerful combinations produce exponential results."
— John H. Zenger and Joseph Folkman

☐ ~~Building strengths is sufficient~~

☑ Fix fatal flaws

Magnifying strengths to the fullest has been one of the main messages so far. In the process, we may have implied that weaknesses should never be the focus of a personal development plan. However, in many cases, focusing on weaknesses is absolutely what needs to be done.

As we have already observed, people challenged to improve their leadership effectiveness have an amazingly similar plan for improvement.

1. Assess areas of strength and weakness. Since being really good or even moderately good at something means you don't have to worry about it, immediately scrutinize your low scores.
2. Decide which weakness is most significant, usually because it has the lowest score.
3. Develop a plan of action to address the weakness.

In fact, in some cases, working on a weakness *is* the best approach to improving. If a fatal flaw is not corrected, it will act as a drag on the overall perception of leadership effectiveness. We believe that even one extremely low score will produce a negative halo effect.

Frederick was the director of research for an international pharmaceutical company. A brilliant chemist, he towered over others in his grasp of the technical aspects of the research process. But his personal manner was curt and abrupt. He cut people off in meetings. He rejected suggestions or ideas for procedures that were not his own. The other department heads felt that he failed to listen to their input. After extensive feedback, Frederick began to change the way he treated others. Making changes in this one specific arena caused his overall ratings to escalate. Conclusion: if you have a fatal flaw, fix it.

An analysis of our data reveals five patterns of behavior that consistently lead to a failure in leadership. Possessing one or more of these virtually makes it impossible for a person to be perceived as an effective leader:

1. Inability to learn from mistakes
2. Lack of relationship-building skills
3. Lack of openness to new ideas
4. Lack of accountability
5. Lack of initiative

The next five lessons examine each of these fatal flaws and what must be done to fix them.

To combat fatal flaws:

Reflect on your experience: What have you learned from past events? Specifically, what did you learn from things that did not go well? What would you have done differently? What will prevent the same thing from happening again?

Assess whether you have any fatal flaws: Get feedback. Participate in a developmental survey to get a good overview of any weaknesses. Are any of your low scores on our list?

Make a specific plan: After reading the following five lessons, you will have a better idea of exactly how to remedy fatal flaws.

"The real fault is to have faults and not try to mend them."

—Confucius

☐ ~~Show no weakness~~

☑ **Learn from mistakes**

Some leaders show such promise that they are expected to go all the way to the top of their organizations—but then something happens to make them fall off the track. These "derailed executives" have been the subject of some fascinating research.

Morgan W. McCall, Jr., and Michael Lombardo found that derailed executives make about the same number of mistakes as those whose careers continue onward and upward, but derailed executives *do not use setbacks or failure in an assignment as a learning experience*. They hide their mistakes from others. They do not take immediate steps to rectify what they have done. And they tend to brood about the mistake, constantly reliving it for years afterward.

Those whose careers continue to soar do exactly the opposite. They readily acknowledge what happened, alert colleagues to the potential consequences, do their best to fix it, and then proceed to forget about it and move on in their career. Our research confirms that *the inability to learn from mistakes is the single biggest cause of failure for leaders*. This is the first fatal flaw.

We can only speculate about the reasons for this. Is failure to learn from mistakes a symptom of not being willing or able to face reality, because it is painful? Does it show that people are unwilling to accept the fact that they could have done something wrong? Or do people genuinely not recognize the serious consequences of what they have done, believing instead, "That problem I had was no big deal. It doesn't really matter"? Perhaps people have never learned the skill of objectively analyzing their own behavior.

A CEO with a brilliant mind and many accomplishments had one fatal flaw. He made hasty decisions about whether to promote people, dismissing some as being incompetent after a 20-minute interview and promoting others because of one thing they had done or said. Despite countless warnings, the CEO selected as his VP of finance an executive with a terrible reputation for backstabbing and sinister political behavior. Eventually, the VP was successful in ousting the CEO, through an end run to the board. Several people commented, "We tried to tell him, but he would not listen." This CEO failed to change course, even after his mistakes were staring him in the face.

To best learn from mistakes:

Review past actions without cringing: Look back and examine what's happened. Where could improvements be made? Recognize that mistakes are part of the learning process. They can be valuable learning tools if you use them that way.

Tell others when you make mistakes: Hiding mistakes only makes their outcome worse. Share your pain, and the problem can begin to be solved. Be sure to inform those who will be affected by the mistake!

Solve the problem: Seek good advice from others you trust. Make adjustments. Then don't relive the past. Once you fix your mistake, move on.

"The team that makes the most mistakes wins."
—John Wooden

☐ ~~Competence is what matters~~

☑ **Build positive relationships**

One of the authors was having dinner with a friend who is currently a university president. When asked about what kinds of activities filled his day, he commented, "Well, today I had to fire a professor." Someone at the table asked, "Why? Was he incompetent?" "No," replied the president, "He was very current in his field! The problem was that no one in his department could remember a staff meeting that he attended that did not end in an argument. He was absolutely impossible to get along with and created so much friction in the department that nothing was getting done." In this case, the professor's lack of interpersonal skills made his other skills irrelevant.

This story highlights the second fatal flaw, which is the inability to build positive relationships. This flaw springs from two major sources: what we do wrong (errors of commission) and what we fail to do right (errors of omission).

Errors of commission. When leaders are abrasive, insensitive, browbeating, cold, arrogant, and bullying, this is a pattern that surely leads to failure in today's world. That behavior was tolerated 50 years ago, but seldom today. No combination of intelligence, hard work, business acumen, and administrative skills can compensate for this interpersonal ineptness. In the human resources profession, the saying goes: "We hire people for their technical competence and fire them for their interpersonal incompetence."

Errors of omission. We are often stunned to see the number of people in middle management positions in organizations who do not follow some of the most rudimentary social rules:

- When you talk to people, look them in the eye.
- Learn and use people's names.
- When talking with people, say or do things that let the other person know you are listening and understanding.
- Do not dominate the conversation and take all the "air time."
- Sincerely inquire about others' ideas and activities.
- Laugh at others' jokes and attempts at humor.

- Praise others' hard work and efforts in furthering a good cause.
- Smile when meeting and greeting other people.

Ways to build productive relationships:

Ask for feedback: It is the golden path to continual improvement. Accept feedback as the valid perceptions of others and seek to understand the meaning. Assume that the givers have pure, positive intent. Resist the impulse to retaliate.

Enroll in developmental experiences: The key is to move outside your comfort zone and do something that will provide real development. Invest in yourself. Take the necessary time off the job to attend.

Practice, practice, practice: Pick one skill to improve upon at a time. Keep a pocketful of pennies. Try to practice that skill 10 times a day. To help keep track, every time you use that skill, shift a penny from one pocket to the other.

"Being interpersonally inept inevitably sinks leaders."

—John H. Zenger and Joseph Folkman

☐ If it ain't broke, don't fix it

☑ Be open to new ideas

Leaders are often beset by twin demons—arrogance and complacency. Arrogant leaders believe their ideas are superior to everyone else's. Complacent leaders are simply unwilling to listen to others' ideas and experiment with them. They are content with the status quo.

Perhaps these leaders feel threatened by good ideas coming from others. Maybe they lack the energy to make changes. Maybe they grew up with the mistaken notion that those with the formal title of "manager" should have the answers to all problems.

This lack of openness to new or different ideas is the third fatal flaw. It can be a major turnoff to subordinates. Insisting on doing things the same old way can have two major negative consequences.

1. **Impact on subordinates:** People feel ignored, their ideas unappreciated, and their contribution undervalued. Under such leaders, morale degenerates and turnover escalates.
2. **Impact on the organization:** Good ideas and solutions fail to get implemented. Because good ideas are squelched, people stop thinking about better ways to do things. The organization stagnates.

Many consulting firms have developed a successful practice by interviewing employees and seeking their opinions and recommendations about the serious issues the organization faces. The consulting firm then presents these ideas to upper management, along with a hefty bill. The fact is, the employees would have been willing to tell the executives exactly the same things, had the executives asked. Many employees have told us that they and their coworkers have usually tried to pass on those messages, but no one was listening. The great ideas are there—if leaders will seek them out.

One senior executive shared his techniques for dealing with people who come to him with new ideas. He said, "I don't ever discourage a new idea. Ideas are tender and need to be nourished. So I ask lots of questions and give the person encouragement to pursue it, unless I'm positive it won't work. If I have the slightest belief it could succeed, I am enthusiastic about it. Over the years, that's paid off in some remarkable advancements."

Here are some ways to cultivate a climate that welcomes new ideas:

Ask people for their thoughts: Your best resources are all around you. Ask the people closest to the work for their ideas about how to do things better.

Shower ideas with enthusiasm: Give people an opportunity to think out loud. Ask them for details. Even if you can't implement an outrageous idea, sometimes the process will lead to a better alternative.

Infuse energy in the process: Let people know you will not let their ideas drop. Leaders need to capture and amplify the enthusiasm of others.

"Many of us have worked for leaders whose automatic response to every idea or suggestion was negative. It is impossible to calculate the damage such a person does inside an organization."
— **John H. Zenger and Joseph Folkman**

☐ Make a good impression

☑ Be accountable

Some managers seem to subscribe to the philosophy, "It doesn't matter if you win or lose, it's how you place the blame." These managers have fallen prey to the fourth fatal flaw—lack of accountability. Leaders who do not assume complete responsibility for the performance of a work group are bound to fail.

The accountable leader, on the other hand, identifies so strongly with the group that *the success of the work group equals personal success*. The responsible leader puts organizational goals ahead of personal ambitions and puts the welfare of the total organization ahead of his or her own department. The responsible leader does things for which there may be no immediate reward, but does them because they are the right thing to do and will help the organization in the long run.

Leaders must be accountable in their dealings with the following groups:

Behavior with subordinates: Responsible leaders take complete charge of the group, never shirking decisions by wishing to remain "one of the group." They insist that individuals live up to their responsibilities. They are willing to terminate poor performers when necessary, understanding that the performance of the group is more important than salving the feelings of one person. Responsible leaders don't hesitate to take blame for failures but never fail to pass along credit for high-quality work. They invite subordinates to make presentations on the team's success to senior executives, to give them exposure and experience.

Behavior with upper management: Accountable leaders accept criticism for mistakes. They buffer their group from excessive criticism. They tenaciously ensure that the group meets the expectations of upper management. In circumstances where the work group is being held up by management indecision, the responsible leader must sometimes take a risk and press the executives to make timely choices.

Behavior with other groups: Responsible leaders do not let anything fall in the cracks between their group and other departments, suppliers, or customers. Instead of shrugging their shoulders and saying, "It is not my responsibility," accountable leaders say, "If it is not someone else's clear responsibility, then we'll do it."

Taking responsibility means being willing to do the following:

Shift your mindset: Think in new ways about your responsibilities. Keep the big picture in mind. Visualize ways to get the organization where it needs to be.

Take the heat: You don't need to take responsibility for every bad event, but honestly evaluate what you could have done to prevent any failures. At the same time, heartily sing your workers' praises. Never miss an opportunity to tell others of the good work being done by the people around you.

Remember you're the boss: Sometimes it's up to you to do the unpopular thing. You may need to fire unproductive workers or push people to do better work. It's more important to be effective than liked.

"Management has no power. Management has only responsibility."

—Peter F. Drucker

☐ ~~Fulfill your~~ assignment

☑Take initiative

The fifth fatal flaw is the failure to make things happen. Aspiring leaders who lack initiative drive a huge nail into their own career coffins. Leaders must create results. They must be on the forefront of creating needed change.

One measure of a leader's effectiveness is the number of initiatives he or she personally champions. What projects has this leader started? What outcomes have this leader's fingerprints all over them? What has happened that would not have occurred had this leader not been present?

The leader with initiative stops to consider the current reality and asks questions such as these:

- What is missing that would make a big difference?
- What needs to be done that only I can do?
- What could I do that would make a significant difference to the performance of this work team?

If I had to pick one action step, what would it be?

■ What are others expecting me to do?

This leader then steps in and makes those things happen. This is a totally different approach from the leader who waits and responds to events after they happen. Action-oriented leaders must act like surfers. They need to be positioned in front of the wave to get a thrilling ride. Surfers who are a second too slow simply bob up and down in the ocean waiting for the next wave. Getting out in front is where extraordinary leaders must be.

We recommend that leaders take the initiative to implement a change in their organizations. The change could be as simple as implementing a new reporting system or as complicated as a new organizational structure. As Machiavelli noted, "There is nothing more difficult to carry out, nor more doubtful of success, nor more dangerous to manage, than to initiate a new order of things." But nothing builds leadership skills so effectively as the process of initiating change.

Taking initiative requires the following steps:

Study the organizational landscape: What changes are needed? Where should the organization be? Think several steps ahead.

Make an action plan: Determine what outcomes you plan to achieve and how you plan to achieve them. After implementing the change, evaluate how well the change succeeded. What would work better next time?

Don't wait for more responsibility—take it: In one of the best studies of powerful developmental experiences, Anna Valerio concluded that nothing has more impact on a leader's development than being given a broader scope in his or her current assignment. Broader responsibility can be granted, or it can be self-generated. Try applying for a new technology transfer, implementing a new procedure, or volunteering to do more.

"You can't build a reputation on what you are going to do."

—Henry Ford

☐ Listen to yourself

☑ **Learn from feedback**

Inside everyone's head is a picture of how they see themselves. This mental self-portrait sums up their values, behaviors, and self-image. In most cases, leaders with a fatal flaw are totally unaware of that flaw. For example, people who immediately reject others' ideas would probably describe themselves as having such extensive experience that they know what ideas will succeed and fail. These individuals don't know they are perceived as rejecting everyone else's ideas. How can that be changed?

Feedback from coaching, team discussions, or 360-degree surveys can provide "disconfirming information." The messages conveyed would be contrary to leaders' self-perceptions. This creates a dilemma and forces action. Leaders now have several choices:

First, deny the information. But if it comes from multiple sources that are clearly reliable, it becomes extremely difficult to deny this consistent pattern of feedback.

Second, choose to change their self-concept. Leaders can say to themselves, "OK, I guess I am arrogant and think my ideas are the only good ones that exist." However most would find this unacceptable and illogical.

Third, change behavior. For most people faced with a barrage of disconfirming information, the easiest course of action is actually to change the behavior. That is the power of feedback.

Not all feedback is equally useful. Feedback is most valuable if it is specific, focused, and related to the behavior or process rather than general personality characteristics. The most useful feedback focuses on the intensity of effort, the innovative approaches used, or the ability to overcome obstacles. If a child is told, "Wow, you really worked hard on that," he or she will be better equipped to face future challenges than if told, "Wow, you're really smart." This is a subtle difference in the way feedback is given, but it can powerfully affect the way people view themselves and their abilities.

Not all people like the same type of feedback. Some people are highly motivated by positive feedback. They feel crushed by negative feedback. However, other people are skeptical of positive feedback because they care most about averting failure. To them, negative feedback is a source of useful information, while positive feedback comes across as hollow praise.

The fine art of learning from feedback will be easier if you do the following:

Find trustworthy sources of feedback: It's easy to get blindsided by our own weaknesses. We need people we can trust who will tell us the truth about ourselves. Don't shy away from giving good feedback to others.

Stick with specifics: Excellent feedback gives people specific information. Give detailed examples where possible. Describe what actually happened rather than your assumptions about the events.

Tailor feedback to the person: Be sensitive. If the person's life orientation is to prevent disaster, stick with suggestions for improvement to help him or her achieve that goal. If individuals will be devastated by negative feedback, accentuate the positive aspects of their performance.

"Not to know is bad; not to wish to know is worse."

—African proverb

☐ Set up a frontal assault

☑ Take a nonlinear approach

Warfare through the 1700s to the middle of the nineteenth century was characterized by two groups of soldiers marching in rows straight toward each other. Not until the American Revolution did soldiers begin hiding behind trees and lying on the ground to avoid being easy targets. This was an entirely different type of war. We propose a similarly radical approach to developing leadership skills.

If you were to decide to improve a leadership skill, such as your level of technical expertise, you might examine your current performance and determine a list of actions, such as:

1. Sign up for a class.
2. Attend professional workshops.
3. Read technical/professional journals.
4. Read the latest books in the technical/professional field.

5. Broaden your network/ask for coaching or mentoring on specific topics.

This tactic is a classic, linear, frontal assault. This plan plots a straight line from where you are to where you want to be. It is extremely logical and characteristic of many people's propensity to identify a challenge, put their heads down, and run straight at it full force. Our claim is that linear plans work best for people moving from poor performance to good performance. However, moving people from good to great is best accomplished with a nonlinear approach.

Let's examine what a nonlinear path might look like. As we have mentioned previously, certain leadership skills are linked together as what we call "competency companions." *We propose that the best way to make improvements in one skill is sometimes to make improvements in the competency companion skill, not the targeted skill itself.*

For example, if you wanted to develop greater technical competence, you could focus directly on improving that skill, but you might have more success with improving your technical competence if you focus on its "competency companion," which is interpersonal skills. Robert Kelly found evidence for the usefulness of this nonlinear approach in his research on the most productive scientists at Bell Labs. The most competent scientists did not end up being those with the highest IQ or most knowledge. They were the ones who used interpersonal skills to get their work done. They helped colleagues, showed concern, asked others for ideas, and gave others credit.

To benefit from a nonlinear approach:

Change your mindset: The best way to improve in one area may be to ignore it! Instead, you may do better to focus on a related area of improvement.

Build your awareness of competency companions: You will need to know which skills are interrelated in people's minds as characteristics of effective leaders. To find out more about the *Competency Companion Development Guide* by Zenger and Folkman, contact the authors at info@expgi.com.

Savor the side effects: Developing competency companions can change a person. Just as learning to play golf gives you increased confidence, so strengthening a competency can change your perspective and outlook on life, making you more effective in many areas.

"There is no such thing as working on only one leadership quality or attribute. When you improve one, you will invariably be improving several others."
—John H. Zenger and Joseph Folkman

☐ ~~Rest on your laurels~~

☑ Take steps to improve leadership skills

Every aspiring leader can take steps to improve. One of the best places to start is to understand what you do well and capitalize on it. Peter Drucker argued, "Self-development is *making oneself better at what one is already good at*. It also means *not worrying about the things one cannot be good at*." To do this, Drucker advised taking an inventory of major accomplishments in the recent past.

- List your major contributions to the organization over the past two or three years.
- Specify precisely the things the organization expects from you.
- Be clear about what you cannot do as well as what you can do.

By listing past successes, you will have a better understanding of where you are likely to make significant contributions in the future. Think back to high school and college. Let's assume you were extremely adept at mathematics but you did not enjoy language study much nor did you do well at it. Which path should you choose going forward? Do you work hard at becoming better at language? Or do you decide to leverage your talents in mathematics and excel in that area?

We believe it makes sense for you to lead with your areas of strength. No one can do everything. You will feel more motivation, make more progress, and experience more success if you focus on areas that you like and in which you do well. Sometimes the best strategy is to play to your strengths and find ways for others to fill in the gaps. Through delegation, the use of outside resources, or reallocation of work assignments, you can find ways to make your weaknesses irrelevant.

Another excellent strategy for becoming an extraordinary leader is to observe expert leaders around you. Watch how they handle tough situations, particularly when they do it right. Many organizations are not leaving this process to chance these days. They are hiring professional coaches to give objective, constructive feedback to senior leaders. The higher people move in the organization, the less apt they are to hear the truth from people about them, so the value of coaches may increase as people move to higher levels.

Some steps you can take to develop your leadership abilities:

Take stock of your strengths: Don't waste time trying to be something you're not. Become world class in your area of expertise.

Look around for the high performers: See what they're doing. Ask questions. Copy their actions.

Try out leadership skills in other settings: Volunteer in your community. Practicing leadership in other aspects of your life allows you additional opportunities to hone and perfect your skills.

"There are times when a man should be content with what he has, but never with what he is."
—William George Jordan

☐ ~~Focus on the work~~

☑ **Develop your people**

Leaders cast a significant shadow in the their organizations. We have found that employees who have worked for the same boss for several years tend to share not only the strengths but also the weaknesses of their boss. This cuts both ways—if you are an extraordinary boss, your subordinates are likely to develop these skills, but the areas in which they need to improve will also tend to mirror yours.

A powerful tool in your own development process is to develop the people around you. Some leaders view people development as a frill—extraneous to their "real work." However, taking the time to develop people is an important behavior of a leader, not only for what it does for the people he or she helps, but equally for the impact it has on the leader and the organization. Developing others moves you from being an independent professional person, concerned only with yourself, to the role of the true leader who creates organizational capacity and builds people.

Some of the following strategies will help in your efforts to develop those around you:

1. Set high expectations for leaders. By getting your best leaders to excel, everyone benefits.
2. Build "personal dashboards" to monitor the effectiveness of those around you. How do your people know that they are performing well? If no objective measures exist currently, take the initiative to develop them. Better yet, encourage others to develop those measures for themselves.
3. Involve your leaders as teachers. One of the best ways to learn something is to teach it. Engaging leaders to teach new skills to their groups not only solidifies that knowledge, but also builds skills in the leaders and lends credibility to what is being taught.
4. Make development a longer-term process, not an event. We strongly advocate making development part of ongoing work activities rather than a shorter weekend, a weeklong, or even a multi-week program off the job. We are reminded of the executive who asked his boss about attending a 13-week executive development program, to which the boss replied, "If I can spare you for 13 weeks, I can spare you."

5. Celebrate successes. When positive results are achieved, celebrate them. When measures of effectiveness show success, broadcast them widely.

Some good strategies for helping others reach their potential:

Believe in your people: The success of these measures hinges on your beliefs. If you believe your leaders can become extraordinary, they will rise to the challenge.

Expect change to happen sooner rather than later: Leadership is all about change, so if change is not happening, it probably is not working.

Act on your beliefs: Real learning shows up in new behavior. Pick a person. Pick a concept to apply. Start Monday morning.

"The conventional definition of management is getting work done through people, but real management is developing people through work."
—Agha Hasan Abedi

"Great leaders are not defined by the absence of weakness, but rather by the presence of clear strengths. The key to developing great leadership is to build strengths."

"Extraordinary leaders take personal responsibility for the outcomes of the group."

"An extraordinary leader acknowledges a mistake, alerts colleagues to potential consequences, does his or her best to fix it, and then proceeds to forget about it and move on towards success."

The McGraw-Hill Mighty Manager's Series

How to Manage Performance
24 lessons to improve performance
by Robert Bacal
ISBN 13: 978-0-07-711623-1
ISBN 10: 0-07-711623-2

Arms you with proven techniques for inspiring breakthrough productivity levels and infusing both you and your employees' careers with renewed commitment and success.

How to Plan and Execute Strategy
24 steps to implement any corporate strategy successfully
by Wallace Stettinius, D Robley Wood Jr, Jacqueline L Doyle, John L Colley Jr
ISBN 13: 978-0-07-711622-4
ISBN 10: 0-07-711622-4

Provides you with 24 practical steps for creating, implementing, and managing market-defining, growth-driving strategies.

The Handbook for Leaders
24 lessons for extraordinary leadership
by John H Zenger, Joseph Folkman
ISBN 13: 978-0-07-711624-8
ISBN 10: 0-07-711624-0

This precise, no-nonsense rulebook shows you how and why to focus on your core strengths instead of correcting your weaknesses. It outlines the essential competencies and guidelines for effective leadership.

Managing in Times of Change
24 tools for managers, individuals and teams
by Michael Maginn
ISBN 13: 978-0-07-711625-5
ISBN 10: 0-07-711625-9

Shows how to help your workforce realize the benefits of change and flourish within their new environment and responsibilities.

How to Motivate Every Employee
24 proven tactics to spark productivity in the workplace
by Anne Bruce
ISBN 13: 978-0-07-711619-4
ISBN 10: 0-07-711619-4

Tips for motivating your workforce for their own careers and the long-term success of your business.

Dealing with Difficult People
24 lessons to bring out the best in everyone
by Rick Brinkman, Rick Kirschner
ISBN 13: 978-0-07-711620-0
ISBN 10: 0-07-711620-8

Disarm problem people, find common ground and turn conflict into cooperation.

The Sales Success Handbook
20 lessons to open and close sales now
by Linda Richardson
ISBN 13: 978-0-07-711621-7
ISBN 10: 0-07-711621-6

Outlines a battle-tested program for hearing and understanding exactly what your customers have to say and selling solutions instead of just selling products.

About the Authors

John H. (Jack) Zenger, D.B.A., is executive vice-president and director of Provant, Inc., and the author or coauthor of number of books on the principles of leadership, including *The Extraordinary Leader* and *Results-Based Leadership*.

Joseph Folkman, Ph.D. is managing director of Novations Group, Inc., and the author of *Turning Feedback Into Change, Making Feedback Work,* and *Employee Surveys That Make a Difference*.